WRITE YOUR NAME IN RUNES

THIS BOOK BELONGS TO

Before you can fill this in you need to know a little about Anglo-Saxon writing. They used letters called *Runes*. You can see them below. Underneath are the letters we use today. Now you can work out how to write in runes:

f u th o r k g w h n i j h p x s t b e ng m l d œ a æ y ea

How can you tell that the runes were often carved – on wood, stone or ivory?

Sometimes they thought runes were like magic. This ring has these letters on it in runes:

ærkriufltkriurithonglæstæpontol

Nobody knows what this means.

You could make up some magic words of your own and write them in runes.

This scene is carved on ivory. There are some runes in a box at the top. Can you work out what they say? What does the picture show?

Answer:

The runes say 'magi'. The picture shows the Three Kings.

Where did the Anglo-Saxons live?

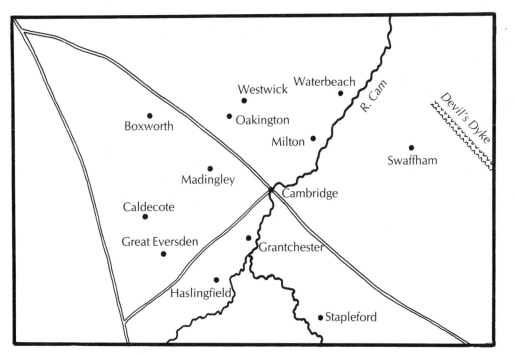

Here is a map of part of Cambridgeshire. To find out where the Anglo-Saxons lived, look for the place-names with:

den, *dene* = hill
feld, *field* = field
ford = river crossing
ham = settlement
lea, *leigh*, *ly* = clearing in the woods
ton = farm or village
wick, *wich*, *wic* = farmstead
worth = land enclosed by a hedge

Underline the Anglo-Saxon names you find on the map.

Look at a map of the area where you live and see if you can find any Anglo-Saxon names.

How else can you find where they lived?
You could look for their buildings.

This is part of an Anglo-Saxon church in Cambridge dedicated to St Benedict.

Some of their houses have been reconstructed from what archaeologists have dug up. This one is at West Stow in Suffolk.

They also built great dykes to keep their enemies out, like Offa's Dyke. This one is called the Devil's Dyke. Can you find it on the map?

How many animals?

There are an awful lot of animals tangled together here. Try to work out how many there are.

Start by finding these two.

What kind of object do you think this is? The answer is below.

Now colour in the animals separately, using a different colour for each one, and see how many there are. It's more tricky than you think!

Here are some more animals all twisted together. Have a go at filling in the gaps. Then colour them in.

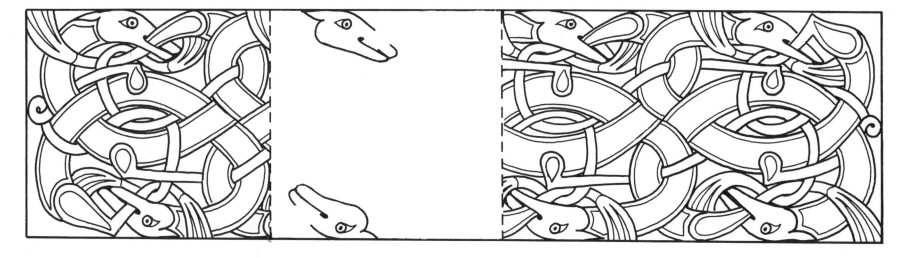

Answer

It is a buckle from a belt, and comes from Sutton Hoo in Suffolk.

An Anglo-Saxon calendar

These are some pictures from Anglo-Saxon manuscripts showing people at work throughout the year. Can you tell what they are doing? There are clues at the bottom of the page.

SOWING   DIGGING   HARVESTING   HAYMAKING   THRESHING   SHARPENING A SCYTHE   CHOPPING TREES   REAPING

WINTER

SPRING

SUMMER

AUTUMN

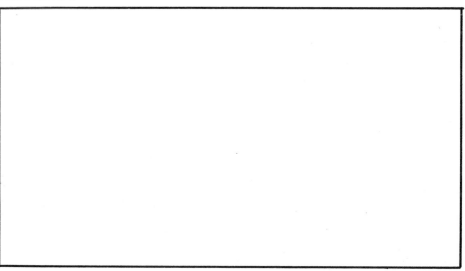

Decide which season of the year each of these pictures belongs to and copy them into the boxes to make your Anglo-Saxon calendar. We have done Winter for you.

You could draw boxes like these onto another piece of paper and make a calendar about life today. Show what you do in spring, summer, autumn and winter. Or you could show what it is like on a modern farm.

How to be an Anglo-Saxon King

You may have come across kings with names like Ethelred, Egbert and Offa – but being an Anglo-Saxon king was no joke. These pictures show some of the things they had to do. What are they? Answers below.

On the back cover is a game where you can be a king.

You could design your own coin like this one; put your name round the edge and REX (for 'king') or REGINA (for 'queen'). Stick your coins onto card and issue them to your friends.

Building ships/defending towns/minting coins/dispensing justice/making laws/giving to the Church

The Battle of Maldon

The Battle of Maldon is the subject of a famous poem. It was fought by Anglo-Saxons and Vikings in Essex in AD 991. The Vikings had camped on an island in the river connected by a causeway to the mainland where the Anglo-Saxons were waiting. The Anglo-Saxon commander, Byrthnoth, gave his men their orders for battle. The Vikings offered a deal: 'It would be better for you to buy off our raid with gold, than that we, known for our cruelty, should cut you down in battle.' Byrthnoth replied scornfully: 'We will pay you in whistling spears, deadly darts and proven swords. Weapons to pay you, pierce, split and slay you in storming battle'.

The Vikings crossed the causeway and the battle began. The poem describes the scene: 'ravens wheeled, eagles were greedy for prey, a wild cry arose from the earth. Warriors slung their razor-sharp spears, shields were pierced with arrows. Fierce was the rush of battle. Soldiers fell on all sides.'

The battle was won by the Vikings, and the Anglo-Saxon commander killed.

Why not draw a picture of part of the battle or show it stage by stage as a cartoon. We've given you some Anglo-Saxon and Viking soldiers to copy.

This map shows the scene of the battle. Mark on it where the two armies were and where the battle took place.

What would you have done in Byrthnoth's place?

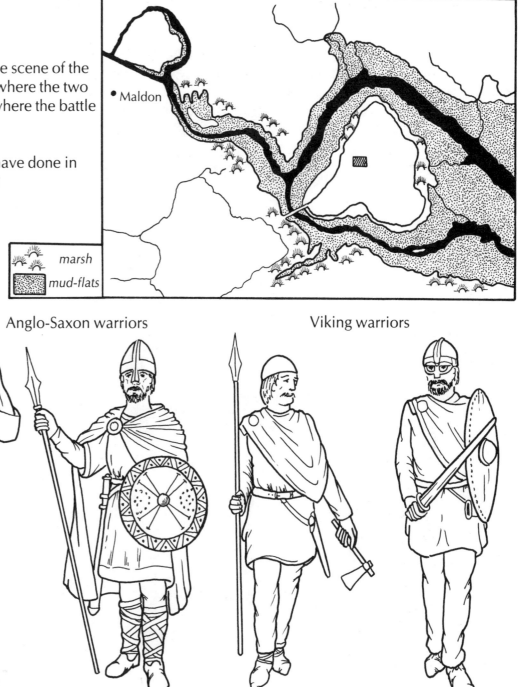

• Maldon

marsh

mud-flats

Anglo-Saxon warriors

Viking warriors

Manuscripts

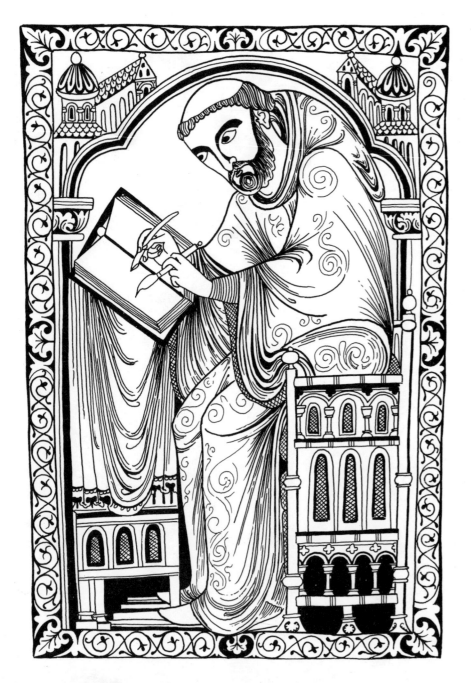

This monk is working on a manuscript – that means 'written by hand'. How can you tell he is a monk?

In his right hand he holds a stylus to write with. What will he do if he makes a mistake?

Instead of paper he is writing on vellum made from specially prepared animal skins. We know that one very big book used the skins of 50 sheep.

Colour this picture in with bright colours – such as red, purple, blue, yellow, green and gold – like the Anglo-Saxons used.

Why not draw a picture like this showing someone writing a book today? Show what they would use and put in modern furniture. You could draw a decorated frame round it, with modern buildings at the top.

If you look on the next page you will see part of a page from a manuscript.

If you look on the next page you will see part of a page from a manuscript.

Answers

He will scratch out his mistakes with the scraper in his left hand.

You can tell he is a monk because of his special hairstyle, called a tonsure.

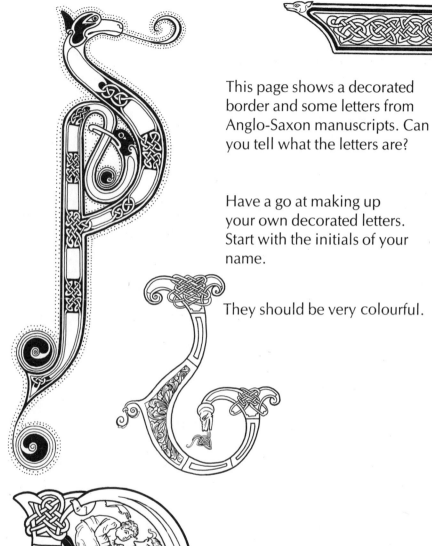

This page shows a decorated border and some letters from Anglo-Saxon manuscripts. Can you tell what the letters are?

Have a go at making up your own decorated letters. Start with the initials of your name.

They should be very colourful.

On the right is a page from an Anglo-Saxon manuscript but its decoration is missing. See if you can finish it off – the patterns on this page should give you some ideas. Then colour it in.

This shows David killing Goliath.

This page comes from the Lindisfarne Gospels. Do you know what language it is written in?

An Anglo-Saxon mystery

This is a picture of an Anglo-Saxon buried in a ship near the coast, at Sutton Hoo in Suffolk, over 1300 years ago. But we don't know who he was.

We can tell a lot about him from what is buried in the ship. What clues can you find?

Now turn to the next page.

What do you think?

Was he a monk, a soldier, or a king?

Can you find anything that could belong to a king?
What might he have worn instead of a crown?

Some of these objects are
decorated with
gold and
silver.

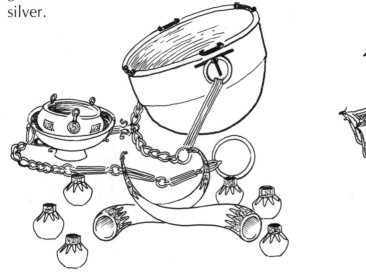

We don't know what this is. It might
have been a standard, or a lamp.
What else do you think it could
have been?

Swords were very precious and
often had names.

There were pictures of fighting men
on the helmet.

Why do you think they buried these things?

There is a description of a similar burial in an Anglo-Saxon poem
called Beowulf.

There in the harbour stood the ice-prowed ship,
the prince's vessel, shrouded in ice and eager to sail;
and they laid their dear lord,
the giver of rings, deep within the ship,
by the mast in majesty; many treasures
and adornments from far and wide were gathered there.

The man buried at Sutton Hoo may have been King Redwald, whom
we know about from a history book written by a monk called Bede.

Jewellery

Wealthy Anglo-Saxon men and women wore splendid jewellery. It is often made of gold, and sometimes decorated with glass or coloured stones. They especially liked garnets (red stones).

Colour in this pendant and clasp.

This is a lady's gold pendant. It is decorated with garnets.

This clasp was found at Sutton Hoo. It is decorated with garnets, and mosaics of blue and white glass.

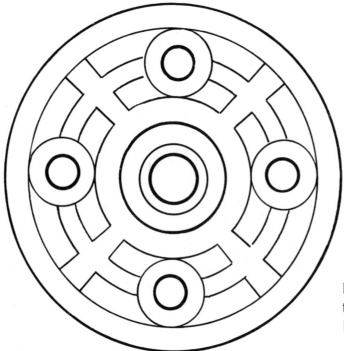

Now you can start to design your own jewellery. This is the gold part of a brooch, but it hasn't been decorated yet. Draw in your own decoration and colour it in.

Fashion

There are five people in the middle of this brooch. They represent the five senses — sight, hearing, smell, taste and touch. Can you tell which is which?

The brooch is not finished yet. The empty circles should have pictures of people, animals, birds and flowers, like the ones we have drawn at the side. Copy these pictures into the circles to complete the brooch, or make up some new ones of your own.

A picture to colour.

One Anglo-Saxon monk described women's fashions: they wore colourful tunics, with silk borders on the sleeves and head-dresses, and red leather shoes. They had long veils on their heads; they curled their hair, and sharpened their finger-nails like hawks' claws!

Dragons and Monsters

This dragon was an ornament on a shield.

One of the greatest Anglo-Saxon poems has lots of monsters and dragons. It tells how the 'grim and greedy' monster Grendel raids the King's hall at night, eating the warriors as they lie asleep, drunk after their feasting. The hero Beowulf slays the 'creature of evil', as Grendel is called, but the following night Grendel's mother, the 'she-wolf of the deep', erupts furious from the lake in which she lives to seek vengeance for her son's death. Beowulf pursues her into the lake, with his magic sword, and after a fierce battle he kills her.

Many years later Beowulf, who is now a king himself, has to face a dragon, which has been terrorising the countryside. A golden cup has been stolen from the dragon's hoard, and so he flies out at night, enraged, and sets fire to the fields and villages. Beowulf seeks the dragon, but he has been mortally wounded in the battle and dies. Sorrowfully, his people bury him in a barrow with treasure, and light a funeral pyre .

Draw a picture illustrating part of the Beowulf story. Or make a 'WANTED' poster of one of the monsters: draw its picture and describe what it has done. Say what the reward is.

Colour in the dragons on this page.

You can read about the Beowulf story in books by Rosemary Sutcliffe and Kevin Crossley-Holland.

This was the prow of a ship.

Dragons were very common in Anglo-Saxon art, and they were used in jewellery and as the prows of ships.

This dragon is from a manuscript.

What is it?

Can you guess what these strange-looking objects are?

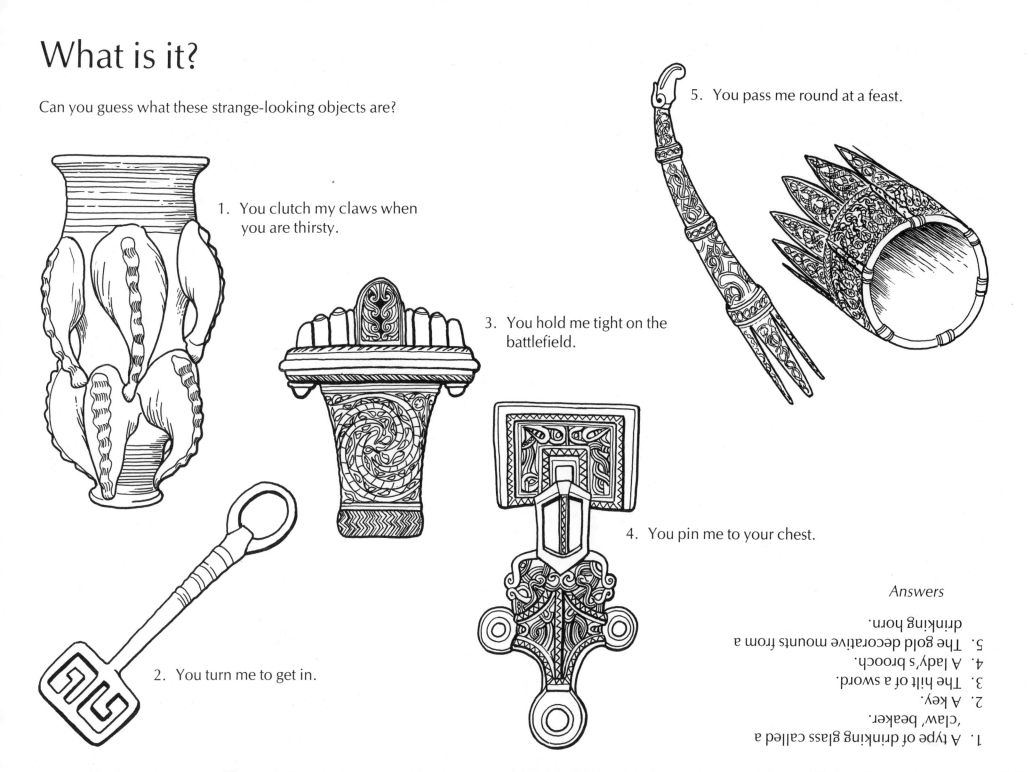

1. You clutch my claws when you are thirsty.

2. You turn me to get in.

3. You hold me tight on the battlefield.

4. You pin me to your chest.

5. You pass me round at a feast.

Feasting

Here is a shopping list for a feast given by a King of Wessex:

10 jars of honey	*20 hens*
300 loaves	*10 cheeses*
12 casks of welsh ale	*a cask of butter*
30 casks of clear ale	*5 salmon*
2 old oxen	*20 pounds weight of hay*
10 geese	

Now make out a menu for the feast on a piece of paper and decorate it.

How many guests do you think there were? What was the hay for? What did the Anglo-Saxons use instead of sugar?

What do you think the people in this picture are eating? Colour the picture in.

Front cover illustration by William Webb

Drawings by Ann Searight

Devised by John Reeve and Jenny Chattington

© 1984 The Trustees of the British Museum

Seventh impression 1991

Published by British Museum Press
a division of British Museum Publications Ltd
46 Bloomsbury Street, London WC1B 3QQ

Typeset by Rowland Phototypesetting Limited,
Bury St Edmunds, Suffolk
and printed in Great Britain by
St Edmundsbury Press Limited,
Bury St Edmunds, Suffolk.